9 Best Ways To Deal With Negative People, Protect Your Health, And Be Happy

Dr. Chio Ugochukwu

**9 Best Ways To Deal With Negative People,
Protect Your Health, And Be Happy**

Published by Bundant Enterprises
3053 Rancho Vista Blvd H-197
Palmdale, CA 93551
**ISBN-13:978-0692568590
(Bundant Enterprises)
ISBN-10:069256859X**

Disclaimer and Terms of Use

The author and publisher have made every effort to ensure the accuracy and completeness of the information contained in this book, we assume no responsibility for errors or omissions therein. It is solely for informational and educational purposes and should not be regarded as a substitute for professional medical treatment, legal, or other professional advice. Your reliance upon information and content obtained through this book is solely at your own risk. The author and publisher assume no liability or responsibility for any adverse consequences for the use of any product, information, idea or instruction contained in this book. Always consult your healthcare provider first.

Dedication

This book is dedicated to all those who would like to protect their health and happiness, from the chronic stressful impact of daily encounters with negative people or negative situations in different aspects of their lives.

Acknowledgement

My gratitude goes to my lovely wife Ekene, and my amazing children for their immense support. I am also thankful to God and to all those who continue to read my books and give me their support and feedback.

Contents

9 Best Ways To Deal With Negative People, Protect Your Health, And Be Happy

Introduction

When dealing with negative people, remember that their aim is to keep you uncomfortable and make you unhappy. In every situation in which you encounter them, they want to put you down and make you do exactly what they want. They may even judge you and hurl hurtful comments at you.

You need to find the best ways to deal with the conflicts and negative feelings that negative people invariably generate either at home, at work or at social gatherings. This is important because though a conflict is simply a disagreement or a difference of opinion between two or more people, it can lead to chronic stress and related health problems, if it is not dealt with immediately.

9 Best Ways To Deal With Negative People, Protect Your Health, And Be Happy

This is because after the initial conflict, most of us end up spending hours worrying about our remarks and reactions to what others have said or done. This is one of the reasons why negative situations or negative people who are difficult to get along with have such a significant impact on our health and our sense of daily happiness.

Negative people are more difficult to get along with because they always want to be right and make a conflict out of almost any issue. This type of person may be viewed as angry and aggressive by others. While these types of situations can be nerve racking and stressful, with the right approach, you can diffuse the related tension, protect your health, and keep yourself calm and happy.

Through this book I will share with you some of the ways you can more effectively handle similar encounters and situations in your life and keep yourself healthy and happy.

Have a strategy for dealing with unexpected encounters with negative persons everyday

No matter where you go in life or who you are, you will encounter negative persons or negative situations in your daily life. Sometimes this will be in the form of negative comments or false accusations. At other times it will be in the form of conflicts. If you do not manage these situations well, they can quickly turn into stressful events that can ruin your day and have a lasting impact on your health.

Having a strategy for dealing with these types of unexpected encounters can help you protect your health and keep yourself happy. Such skills and their regular application can turn out to be the difference between living your daily life with a sense of fulfillment and accomplishment or living with a sense of inadequacy and chronic stress.

One problem with dealing with inherently negative persons is that they seem to enjoy making others uncomfortable. They enjoy making a difference of opinion appear as if it is evidence for incompetence or proof of idiocy. A conflict is different from an argument or fight. Having the right skills to deal with such encounters will help you become more able to turn such differences in opinion or approach into a positive experience for everyone involved.

Negative persons are generally people who are difficult to get along with. They often have poor conflict management skills and have a tendency to make a conflict out of almost any issue. Basically they want to bully you into submission.

The first strategy for dealing with such people is to learn to state your own position or point of view without arguing. Negative people see arguments as a challenge to their authority and they will quickly lash out in explosive anger.

Don't fight fire with fire. Don't get into a shouting match. One skill that you will need to improve to become a better manager of conflicts is the skill of listening. You must have the ability to listen to yourself and to others. Ask questions that show you have been listening. This will help you identify the key elements of the situation while ignoring outlandish comments. Once you do this, you can then make the decision on how you will deal with the situation.

You can do this by either walking away from the situation or by making a strategic decision to stay and change tactics. You can begin the process by maintaining a calm appearance and refusing to internalize negative comments about yourself by repeating them. Instead say, "No".

You also have to learn to avoid turning a negative situation into a battle, where the last one standing is declared the winner. This approach leads to resentments after the fact that can be carried over to future encounters. Aim to have a strategic goal of helping yourself and the negative people, you encounter, walk away happy with the outcome.

Learn to manage your expectations when dealing with others

Almost everyone has expectations of what they want for themselves and for those around them. This includes parents having expectations from their children or children from their parents or friends from their friends. This also extends to the workplace and our daily interactions with others. Can these expectations be so high that they start to cause conflicts within your family, friends and daily interactions with others?

Certain expectations are natural for everyone and include things like wondering what your day will be like, or what the future will bring. While it is great to have expectations they can also cause stress or unhappiness if they are not properly managed. You may end up dumping the ensuing stress on yourself and others.

It is important not to let your expectations get out of hand when dealing with negative people since this can cause real problems. While many expectations are based on reality there are those that are based on our fantasies and our desire to control others. Unfortunately these are the ones that often cause conflicts during our daily interactions with others.

This type of conflict is made worse by negative people because there is no middle ground in their point of view or demands during specific interactions. It is either everything is great or everything is terrible. **The key to staying happy or unruffled during such interactions is to remember that you cannot control how others will behave towards you, but you can control how you would react towards their behavior**.

One way to do this is to lower your expectations when dealing with negative people. Do not expect a negative person to have a positive outlook or a grumpy person to be nice and welcoming towards you.

The critical step that will help you to protect your health and stay happy during your daily interactions with negative people or when dealing with negative situations is to make moment by moment adjustments. Unless we can consistently do this, we shall end up being stressed out and unhappy.

Another approach to the idea of managing expectations when dealing with others may be to lower them and make them more realistic. By turning your expectations into achievable goals you can help avoid conflicts.

This can be done in different situations by setting boundaries and creating avenues through which everyone is allowed to discuss their expectations or goals. Everyone will benefit and this will encourage all parties to the discussion to work towards their different goals, without ever having to worry about conflicts.

9 Best Ways To Deal With Negative People, Protect Your Health, And Be Happy

If you prepare your mind for negative encounters, a more positive one will be not be stressful. However, if you have high expectations of a positive encounter with others, a more negative one will turn out to be very stressful for your health and could significantly diminish your sense of fulfillment and happiness.

Be calm and stay in the present moment so that you will remain effective when you are challenged by a negative person

When dealing with a negative person or negative situation, you need to keep your emotions in check, so that you do not become so angry that you cause more harm than good. You also have to learn how to make sure that the other person's negativity does not humiliate you. One way to accomplish both is to be calm and stay in the present moment without allowing your emotions to overwhelm you.

Do not expect those around you to speak out in support of your situation. This is because most people are only

19

**interested in what they will gain and are
not interested in defending the truth or
trying to be fair to others**. At other times
people will even laugh at you as you grapple
with a difficult negative situation or join in
the negative condemnation when a negative
person berates you. This sad truth will apply
to your friends, family, co-workers,
supervisors or even total strangers.

Unfortunately, this tendency or mentality
is worsened when dealing with negative
persons, who seem to operate on a short
fuse. You will be surprised to discover that
most people will be reluctant to speak up
either because they will not want to be
yelled at or because they enjoy watching a
spectacle at another person's expense.

Staying focused in the present moment
will help you remain calm and discover the
best ways to stay effective in the midst of
such a storm. As a little boy, I still
remember how I was laughed at by those
around me, when my plastic soft drink bottle
fell and spilled its content on my way out of
a supermarket in London. The giggles and

20

laughter got louder as I struggled to stop the spill and close the bottle without much success. I got so overwhelmed by my emotions that I tossed the bottle into the nearest trash can and disappeared from the scene. My auntie who was with me at that time consoled me. She then sternly warned me to never ever again, let the laughter and giggles of those around me, determine my future actions in difficult or negative situations.

Luckily for me the price of not being able to be calm and stay in the present moment was simply a soft drink or large bottle of soda, for others it could be their health or life! Research has shown that strong emotions can impair your memory for less emotional events and your memory for information experienced at around the time of a strong emotional event. This means that it is possible for one to forget whether he has taken his narcotic pain medications or not following a strong emotional encounter with a negative person. This can be dangerous because an accidental overdose of

21

a narcotic pain killer can lead to death. Your ability to protect your health everyday and thrive depends on your ability to stay calm and effective in difficult situations.

The first step in this process would be to take note of the things you or others stand to gain or lose from the current situation. When you figure out what a person who is being negative towards you in a given situation hopes to gain, you will know how to adjust your behavior towards that person.

The second step would be to take note of all of the constraints you may have or all the assumptions you may have made when dealing with a negative person or a negative situation or both. If you go to the grocery store expecting to buy a few things and go home quickly, your patience may be tested by someone who may cut in front of you and insist that he had always been ahead of you. In this scenario, when you tried to explain to the person that he needed to go and start at the back of the line, he refused and threatened to fight you while cussing you out. This whole situation was made worse by the fact that no one else on the cue with you would speak out on your behalf, instead they just looked on. What would you do when dealing with this type of negative person?

Though, you may have a good reason to get angry at the person who cut in front of you and those on the line with you, who remained silent, the best way to diffuse this type of situation maybe to keep quiet and let the person stay ahead of you. This will help you save time and get home faster than if you decided to argue for your right to be treated fairly. At other times speaking out firmly may help. It comes down to situational management and your goal of the moment.

Try to understand the assumptions that are driving your decision making process. Sometimes it is these assumptions that obstruct your view of possible solutions. You have to identify which assumptions are valid, and which assumptions need to be addressed or ignored. It pays to remember that whenever you are dealing with a negative situation, there may be more than one solution to the problem you have to address. Act on one reasonable solution, instead of spending all your time looking for the perfect solution. Concentrate more on how to make your chosen solution work than on whether it is perfect or not.

The third step in this process is to try to imagine how you would behave in future negative situations or encounters with negative persons. It is difficult to master situations you have never anticipated or prepared for. Creative thinking exercises can help you be a more creative problem solver or to deal more effectively with negative persons.

Take a piece of paper and write down any word that comes to mind that you think you might use in such situations. Now look at that word then write the first two words that come to your mind. This can go on until you can build a tree of related words. This can help you build up your analogical skills, and fortify your creative processes. Write down what actions you might take because of the words you have written down.

This type of exercise may pay dividends next time you have to deal with a negative person with a similar problem or attitude. Your critical thinking skills may help you discover a solution that might just be staring you right in your face. All it takes to manage your emotions and stay calm when dealing with negative encounters, is just a little creative thinking, some planning, and good situational management.

9 Best Ways To Deal With Negative People, Protect Your Health, And Be Happy

Look beyond the negative persons you encounter and try to understand their assumptions

Different people have different assumptions and motivations. Some people will be nice to you based on how they feel about you or how you make them feel. The problem with dealing with negative people is that they always feel negatively towards you and act negatively towards you. All their assumptions and motivations towards others are negative. This is one of the reasons why most of us find dealing with negative people so frustrating.

In a work environment you are faced with different personalities, attitudes, work ethics and more. In such a situation, you need to learn how to view yourself as the leader who

27

has the ability to deal with people who might be extremely stubborn or negative. No matter how tough a person may seem bad behavior is not acceptable.

You need to learn certain tactics and tips that will help you manage negative people and negative encounters in different settings. **Always keep a positive mindset with a good attitude**. You will need lots of patience when dealing with difficult people. **Remember that you have all that it takes within you to be effective in any situation you find yourself.** Be prepared to step in and take action immediately. **Don't allow a situation to get to a boiling point before attempting to diffuse it.**

When diffusing a situation always use good language and do not revert to swearing or becoming rude. Remember that understanding everyone's assumption and motivation is difficult. You do not want to hurt anyone's feelings and you don't want to belittle people in front of their co-workers, friends or family. **Try not to 'tell off'**

people, instead try to resolve a conflict by using positive reinforcements.

If you use these tips regularly you will find that you can handle conflicts extremely well. You will earn respect as a leader and people will understand that you are working towards the good of everyone involved. More importantly you will end up creating a win-win situation that helps to diffuse tension, reduce stress and protect your health.

You also have to learn through positive self-talk to love yourself and take control of the most challenging negative situations you encounter everyday. Do not worry about whether others will approve or disapprove of your actions because it is not always easy to determine the assumptions that motivate them.

We have to humbly admit that we are willing to make strategic adjustments that will help us cope with frequent negativity in daily encounters. We can begin this process by learning to say nothing even when people are speaking badly about us. This is difficult

29

9 Best Ways To Deal With Negative People, Protect Your Health, And Be Happy

because complaining about others is easier to do than taking constructive action to improve our emotional control.

Instead of lashing out in anger, when we are negatively attacked we have to learn to let go. We have to take action that will protect our ego, fit our circumstances, our abilities and our personalities. This will help us turn our problems into opportunities for growth.

Remember that there is a purpose for every experience you go through in your journey of life. You can also benefit from the encounter by choosing when to speak and when not to speak or even when to overlook such an annoying behavior or when to forgive. This approach can be applied to all your other interactions with others.

The problem most of us have is that we do not focus on the positive as we try to accomplish our goals. We simply need to focus on making sure we are doing our best everyday, without letting negative thoughts and negative comments, generated by

30

9 Best Ways To Deal With Negative People, Protect Your Health, And Be Happy

negative people, get into our heads and make us sad.

9 Best Ways To Deal With Negative People, Protect Your Health, And Be Happy

Stay focused on trying to improve everyday through better conflict management

Everyday we all deal with unexpected setbacks or our limitations as human beings. Through our interactions we quickly discover how conflicts with others can quickly arise at work, at play, at home or even at our places of worship. Human beings are unpredictable!

Conflict management is having the ability to recognize and deal with disputes in a rational and balanced way. This applies to conflicts that crop up in business as well as those in your personal life.

When dealing with a conflict it is vital that you face this in a calm manner. Allowing the situation to turn you into a shouting match with a negative person will not get the matter resolved.

One important thing to acknowledge is that not all conflicts have to become an angry dispute. However, when we allow negative people to get under our skins during disputes with them, we lose focus and let our emotions get the better of us. We can turn our conflicts with negative people into a healthy thing, if we stay above the fray and stay focused on our main goals for the day. Your main goal everyday should be protecting your health and increasing your productivity. When you consistently do this everyday, your sense of fulfillment and happiness will follow.

When you think about it, people have to work together and everyone has different opinions, so conflicts are only a natural part of the process. At work you have to share desks, resources, and common goals as well as having to work together with a good attitude. All of these things can be sources of conflicts.

9 Best Ways To Deal With Negative People, Protect Your Health, And Be Happy

If you are dealing with a conflict at work your manager or supervisor needs to be aware of the issue. Usually the person in charge will take responsibility for resolving the conflict. They need to do this in a professional manner and without taking sides. It is the problem and not the personalities of the people that need to be resolved.

Conflicts at work or school can sometimes be managed successfully by making certain changes like moving people to different offices or different parts of the classroom. This approach will not work at home or in certain social situations. This is where skills like learning to talk things through and finally reaching a good understanding and agreement between everyone involved, can be very helpful.

Quite often misunderstandings with negative people can be avoided by improving communications in your own personal relationships. Be open and honest and discuss issues before they turn into a full blown conflict.

9 Best Ways To Deal With Negative People, Protect Your Health, And Be Happy

Take action even when you are not sure of your outcome. Sometimes we are our own worst enemies. We give up before we even try. This happens when every time we get a new idea we then find reasons why it will not work. The end result is that our daily situation gets worse. We reject the simple solutions that could help us overcome our daily stress and continue to look for more complex solutions.

36

9 Best Ways To Deal With Negative People, Protect Your Health, And Be Happy

Action overcomes fear. One of the reasons we find ourselves struggling everyday is that we fail to pause and think about what we are doing. Are you running away from an obstacle, instead of trying to overcome it? Do you analyze too much? Are you afraid of being told, "No?" Keep it simple. Stay focused and take action everyday.

9 Best Ways To Deal With Negative People, Protect Your Health, And Be Happy

Commit yourself to taking daily positive action in negative situations even when you are not sure of your outcome

Do not let your circumstances determine your result. To eliminate daily stress from negative situations or negative people, you have to be committed to taking daily action. This action might be smiling when you are angry, or it might be keeping quiet even when you have a few choice words you would like to say to the negative person that is making you feel miserable.

We all want more. **The more we are nice to people the more people will be nice to us.** Surprisingly this applies to negative people even though the emotional cost may be more. If we really want to become winners today we have to respect people and treat them in such a way that will let them know that we consider them important.

One way to do this is to find something genuinely nice to say to people we meet everyday. It will cost us nothing but the rewards will be outstanding. Unfortunately, most of us are stuck at the level of treating others the way they treat us. This is a natural reaction and it is counter intuitive to treat those who are rude to you nicely.

Unfortunately, this is where most of us make mistakes. We get discouraged. We base our actions towards others on our feelings alone. We forget that being nice to people who are rude to us can turn a negative situation or encounter into a positive experience. **We can do this by saying positive things about others without being naïve.**

When you treat people with respect and dignity, they will feel good about themselves and they will equally treat you with respect. This will help you feel more

9 Best Ways To Deal With Negative People, Protect Your Health, And Be Happy

confident about yourself, more successful, and less stressed out.

Invest your time and energy in treating people positively people. Be thankful and nice even to those who are not nice to you. **Smile without reason**.

9 Best Ways To Deal With Negative People, Protect Your Health, And Be Happy

Use critical thinking to deal with negative situations and the negative people that generate them

When you use critical thinking to solve problems in your personal or business life, you can be much surer of a better outcome. Critical thinking helps you to discard biases and beliefs and statements that are hurled at you through your daily interactions with others.

The first step in using critical thinking to deal with negative situations is to clarify the problem. It will not be enough to know that there is a problem, you need to clarify it. This means you need to know what is causing the problem, what emotions it generates for you and the other person and how you can make positive adjustments.

43

9 Best Ways To Deal With Negative People, Protect Your Health, And Be Happy

The second step in the process means that you have to recognize that unless you can carefully analyze the situation you will end up drawing the wrong conclusion. When you draw the wrong conclusion, you will end up with the wrong solution. You have to be able to look beyond what's presented as "facts" in the situation and seek other perspectives on the matter. Sometimes this will mean keeping quiet when you want to speak, at other times it will mean going with the flow.

The third step in the process is to be open-minded about possible solutions. Sometimes your first impulse when dealing with negative people will turn out to be completely wrong. Be patient enough with yourself to think of the implications of some of your solutions to the problem. Remember that every action you take has the potential to lead to an equal and opposite reaction. **Don't always assume that your kind gestures will always be welcome. It can be misinterpreted**.

9 Best Ways To Deal With Negative People, Protect Your Health, And Be Happy

Look at your past experience to see whether you have dealt with similar encounters successfully in the past. What will be the impact of certain solutions and what research can you perform that will offer accurate answers? This is a good approach if the negative situation is a recurring problem. If it is an acute problem, sometimes the best solution would be to take your best considered action and make further adjustments. After all in a chess game, it is not always possible to know all the moves your opponent could make, before you make your next move.

After carefully considering the advantages and disadvantages of your proposed solutions, choose one and act. This means that if you come across a new idea you haven't considered in the past, don't dismiss it without gathering evidence and weighing the alternatives.

Choose a solution that fits your personality, your world view, your dreams, and your goals. If you do not chose a solution that fits your personality, you will end up, not taking action at all. Have the courage to act instead of waiting for the perfect solution before you act. The more you act, the more confident you will become in similar situations in the future.

Make thankfulness the central theme in your interactions with yourself and others

You have to learn to be thankful for the opportunities and surprises that life presents to you everyday. This has to be the case even when you are dealing with negative people and negative situations. The easiest way to begin this process is to have an attitude of thankfulness throughout your daily moments.

This will help you to stay calm and serene, even when you are dealing with negative people and negative situations that you have not encountered before. You can also stay calm by listening to others and being thankful in your interactions with others. **Don't let the negative situations or the hurtful words from negative people disrupt your thoughts and take away your ability to remain confident and positive.**

Without self-confidence your ability to remain successful and happy will be greatly diminished. One way to counter this tendency is to count your blessing and remain defiantly positive in your outlook. You can be thankful because you can see the blue skies, you can hear the birds singing, you can listen to your favorite music, and you can still remember the names of your children, and find your way to the restroom unassisted.

Being thankful for the ordinary things of daily life is a great way to begin each day. This will help you to focus on what makes you happy, instead of focusing on what makes you sad. Don't allow negative people or negative situations make you focus on sadness and anger. Instead

48

seize the opportunity to start a mantra of "Thank you". It will help you cut down on stress and protect your health.

Be thankful for your car that started this morning. Be thankful you have not been snowed in. Be thankful that the person that is yelling at you is not fighting you. **Be thankful that you can think and take action.** Be thankful that you are free and you can simply get up and leave!

Apart from being thankful to those who help you, you also have to learn to have a thankful attitude towards those who treat you unfairly or try to trample on your rights throughout the day. This is counter-intuitive but it will help you to stay calm, act smart, and avoid reacting in anger during challenging circumstances. By staying calm when dealing with negative people, you will eliminate stress and prevent the release of stress hormones which may harm your body.

Without a consistent attitude of thankfulness towards others and yourself, you shall frequently find yourself caught up in one storm or another as you

navigate through the sea of life. Remember that the only thing constant in life is "change".

Don't get so offended by the negative experiences you are dealing with right now, that you forget that no condition is permanent. An uneducated man can become educated. An uneducated woman can become educated. A poor man or woman can become rich. A sad person can become happy again. **You only have to make the decision to be happy and remain focused on what you can control.** Do not forget that according to Oliver Wendell Holmes, the great purpose of life is to live it!

.

Use your will power when dealing with negative people or negative situations

Getting mad and yelling during your interaction with a negative person may be a reflection of how poorly you have used your will power. Using your will power effectively in challenging circumstances is not easy, but you can take steps that will help you get better outcomes.

One tip that will help you handle negative people better would be to look at your past behavior. If for example, you know that anytime you barely make it to the post office, you always end up getting into time-related arguments with the postal workers, make adjustments. Get there earlier. Use your will power to overcome the distractions that usually make you late.

Secondly have a plan "B", in case you get to the post office with little time to spare. Go out of your way to be polite to the postal worker, but quietly insist on your right to be served to the full extent, if there are no notices stating otherwise.

Train yourself to become better at applying your will power in difficult situations. You can do this by learning to look at your brain as a muscle. The more you use it, the stronger it comes or the better it adapts to negative situations. One way to do this would be to find some unpleasant tasks and complete them. These can be simple things like cleaning the house when you do not feel like doing it, or washing the dishes, when you would rather be watching your favorite movie or making those unpleasant but necessary phone calls.

Every time you successfully carry out these unpleasant or unwanted tasks, congratulate yourself. Every time you interact with a negative person without losing your temper, getting angry or feeling less of a person, put a dime in a special piggy bank. When you do it 100 times, take the ten dollars and give yourself a treat! This type of behavior would help you have confidence in your ability to handle negative people or negative situations.

Finally you have to remember that the way you have behaved in the past in a certain situation, may be a good indicator of how you would behave in the future under similar circumstances. If you find yourself in a situation with people whom you consider negative, who have gotten under your skin and stressed you out in the past, they will probably do the same in the future unless you make adjustments. Without changing our thoughts and actions in such negative situations, we shall not get different results. We can do better and become more.

**9 Best Ways To Deal With Negative People,
Protect Your Health, And Be Happy**

Epilogue

Consider finding the best way to deal with negative people a life-long goal. Remember that some of life's most satisfying experiences are those that involve staying focused on a goal until you achieve it. This means that you should not be surprised if obstacles in all shapes and sizes come your way as you try to deal better with negative people, protect your health and be happy.

Despite reading this book and other books on a similar topic, you may still have your own struggles determining how to best work towards attaining what you want. Perhaps you've become disappointed because previous attempts to apply what you have learned to negative situations had failed. This can lead to negative thinking.

Don't let negative thinking hold you back because we have all been plagued by negative thinking. Remember that action overcomes fear. Be thankful and break up your goals into small projects that can be achieved through small consistent daily actions.

Do not surround yourself with people who are only good at telling you how you will not succeed. Ignore them. Build up confidence and banish negative thoughts by reminding yourself that even if you do not succeed the first time, you can try again and again. **Success favors those who do not give up.**

When things get tight or you fail to get the results you want, it is not unusual for you to seriously question your skill and ability to deal better with negative people and negative situations. Instead of focusing on your past failures and past mistakes, this is the time to remind yourself that you can get better and become more. Remind yourself of your past achievements. Give yourself props for goals you've achieved before. Tell yourself that if you have done it before, you can do it again.

Do not let others discourage you through their distractions or lack of confidence in you. Take responsibility to keep your creativity going. Write down how you want to behave when you are dealing with negative people or when you find yourself in negative situations. Draw pictures of what you hope to achieve. Make a note about how happy you will feel when you finally put yourself in the winning position. Tell yourself, "I will do it."

Remind yourself everyday about why you want to reach a particular goal. It will help you reduce stress and protect your health. Perhaps it will help you cut down on the medications you have to take because of the anxiety or sadness that negative encounters with negative people regularly generate for you.

Stay the course by re-committing to your goals each morning. Don't be overwhelmed,

**9 Best Ways To Deal With Negative People,
Protect Your Health, And Be Happy**

you do not have to do everything at once.
Develop your own ways to remain thankful
and keep your thoughts positive when you
deal with negative people or negative
situations.

Resources

Here are additional resources that will help you protect your health, reduce stress, communicate better, and live a transformed life.

www.compasswellnessinstitute.com

www.compasshealthtransformer.com/members

www.dcompassmarketing.com

www.amenfathermbaka.com

http://www.amazon.com/Dr.-Chio-Ugochukwu/e/B00JNFLPQQ

Other books by Dr. Chio Ugochukwu that will help you improve your health, reduce stress and transform your life include;

9 Best Ways To Deal With Negative People, Protect Your Health, And Be Happy

The Compass Health Transformer: Your 72 Hour Blue Print For Healthy Living

21 Ways To Transform Your Health Without Medications

"…21 simple proven ways to reduce stress and improve your health and wellbeing without relying on medications. These are easy and effective ways you can use to turn your daily challenges into transformative opportunities for healthy living and daily happiness. You can start right away without spending a fortune!.."

Get your own copy of 21 Ways To Transform Your Health Without Medications

The Compass Health Transformer Quit Smoking

Overcoming Daily Stress: 21 Quick And Easy Ways To Stay Stress-Free In Your Daily Life

"…Are you tired of being stressed out everyday? Are you tired of feeling exhausted and overwhelmed in your daily activities? Are you fed up with

60

communication issues in your relationship? Here are 21 quick and easy ways you can use to overcome daily stress and turn your daily challenges into opportunities for transformative abundant living. This book will help you gain a better understanding of your potential communication issues, daily 'stress points' and the steps you can take to overcome them…".

<u>**Get your own copy of Overcoming Daily Stress**</u>

The Secret To Daily happiness

"..Have you ever wondered why daily happiness has continued to elude you? Do you want to make sustainable daily happiness part of your life? By reading this book. you can find answers to these questions and many more on how to overcome the many obstacles and challenges that daily try to take away your inner peace and contentment…"

<u>**Get your own copy of The Secret To Happiness**</u>

15 Simple Ways to lower your blood pressure naturally after 40 without complicated diets

"......Don't spend your most productive years dealing with high blood pressure, medications and side effects. Stop worrying about whether you forgot to take your first medication or the second one. Take these simple steps to lower your blood pressure naturally and minimize your need for multiple medications. Did you know that high blood pressure can cause heart attack, stroke, kidney failure, blindness and memory problems? Don't wait to find out! Take Action! ,,,,,"

Click Here to Your own copy of 15 Simple Ways To Reduce Blood Pressure....

How To Lose 23 Pounds Of Fat Without Torture Diets Or Hard Exercise And Keep It Off (The Compass Method)

Managing Time For Success

Too Young To Die

"A book about coping with grief and finding your way in life..."

**9 Best Ways To Deal With Negative People,
Protect Your Health, And Be Happy**

To order new or additional copies, please visit:

http://www.amazon.com/Dr.-Chio-Ugochukwu/e/B00JNFLPQQ

Call:661 992 6436

You can also get EBOOKS from

www.compasswellnessinstitute.com/Ebooks

**9 Best Ways To Deal With Negative People,
Protect Your Health, And Be Happy**

About the Author

Dr. Chio Ugochukwu has always been interested in helping people improve their health, reduce stress, transform their lives, and become the best versions of themselves. He created the Transformational Abundant Living System (TALS) and developed the Compass Method to help individuals stay healthy and become more. He founded the Compass Research Institute to help individuals and organizations, maximize their strengths and overcome their weaknesses to get the best performance out of themselves, and become more empowered in their search for better health, more success and greater happiness despite their busy schedules, daily activities and duties.

He was inspired to create the TALS and the Compass Method, through the challenges he has encountered in his journey of life, his practice of medicine and his fascination with how the mind, the spirit and human experience influence the fulfillment of life. TALS is available at www.compasswellnessinstitute.com.

As an author and researcher, he has published many books, with peer-reviewed publications on quality of life and numerous articles on transformational living. He is the medical director of Dala Compass Foundation and a consultant with the Compass Research Institute. As a life-long learner, He is focused on sharing with individuals and organizations, customized methods and strategic pathways for getting the best performance for themselves and their organizations.

www.ingramcontent.com/pod-product-compliance
Lightning Source LLC
Chambersburg PA
CBHW071429040426
42445CB00012BA/1312